Rookie
Read-About® Holidays

Diwali

D0249319

By Christina Mia Gardeski

Consultants
Nanci R. Vargus, Ed.D.
Primary Multiage Teacher
Decatur Township Schools, Indianapolis, Indiana

Katharine A. Kane, Reading Specialist
Former Language Arts Coordinator,
San Diego County Office of Education

Children's Press®
A Division of Scholastic Inc.
New York   Toronto   London   Auckland   Sydney
Mexico City   New Delhi   Hong Kong
Danbury, Connecticut

Designer: Herman Adler Design
Photo Researcher: Caroline Anderson
The photo on the cover of this book shows diyas glowing and sparklers
crackling during a Diwali celebration.

Library of Congress Cataloging-in-Publication Data

Gardeski, Christina Mia.
    Diwali / by Christina Mia Gardeski.
      p. cm. — (Rookie read-about holidays)
    Includes index.
    Summary: A simple introduction to the autumnal holiday Diwali, the
Festival of Lights that marks the beginning of the Hindu new year.
    ISBN 0-516-22372-0 (lib. bdg.)   0-516-26311-0 (pbk.)
    1. Divali—Juvenile literature. [1. Divali. 2. Fasts and feasts—Hinduism.
3. Hinduism—Customs and practices. 4. Holidays.] I. Title. II. Series.
BL1239.82.D58 M27   2001
294.5'36—dc21

                                   00-046607

Bang! Crack! Boom!
It must be Diwali
(DEE-wahl-ee)!

November 2004

Sunday	Monday	Tuesday	Wednesday	Thursday	Friday	Saturday
	1	2	3	4	5	6
7	8	9	10	11	12	13
14	15	16	17	18	19	20
21	22	23	24	25	26	27
28	29	30				

Diwali is a holiday
celebrated around the
world by people of the
Hindu (HIN-doo) religion.

Diwali lasts for five days.
It comes in October or
November every year.

Diwali is a happy time.
It marks the beginning
of the Hindu new year.

A city street decorated for Diwali

Many Hindus live in India. Diwali is a very important holiday in that country.

Almost every state in India has a Diwali celebration.

Many towns and cities
have carnivals. People play
games and go on rides.

They dance and listen to
music. Firecrackers light
up the night.

During Diwali, many people remember the story of a good prince named Rama.

Long ago, Rama left his city. He was gone for fourteen years.

13

While Rama was away,
he fought a big battle with
a bad king.

This king was trying to
hurt the people of India.

Rama beat the king. Then
Rama returned to his city.

People lit rows of diyas
(DEE-yahs), or small
clay lamps, to welcome
Rama home.

The lamps reminded
them of Rama's strength
and goodness.

The word Diwali means
row of lights.

Today, Hindus still light diyas during Diwali. They put them all around their homes and businesses.

Families clean and paint their houses to get ready for Diwali.

They place fresh flowers all around.

Some people paint colorful
rangolis (rang-oh-LEEZ),
or pictures, on the walls
and floors of their homes.

They hope these pictures
will bring them good luck
in the new year.

Many people buy new clothes
to wear during Diwali. They
also send cards to relatives.

In India, people buy more cards for Diwali than for any other holiday!

Diwali sweets

Diwali is a time for
family and friends to
come together.

They give gifts, such as
dried fruits, chocolates,
and other sweets.

Many people play
card games.

Families say special prayers
and sing songs. They also
share big meals.

Celebrating Diwali helps
everyone have a happy
new year!

29

Words You Know

carnival

diyas

firecrackers

30

Index

About the Author

Christina Mia Gardeski is a writer and editor of children's books. She is forever grateful to her parents for encouraging her love of reading and writing.

Photo Credits

Photographs ©: Dinodia Picture Agency: 3, 30 bottom right (M. Amirtham), 24 (D. Banerjer), 11 (Sunil S. Kapadia), 29 (R. M. Modi), 20, 31 bottom right (Satish Parashar), 8 (Ravi Shekhar), 14; Panos Pictures: 7, 25 (DAS), 17, 30 bottom left (Dominic Sansoni), 10, 30 top (Paul Smith); The Image Works/Dinodia Picture Agency: 13, 31 top left; Viesti Collection, Inc.: cover (Dinodia Picture Agency), 26, 31 bottom left (Trip), 18, 19 (Joe Viesti); Woodfin Camp & Associates/Lindsay Hebberd: 23, 31 top right.

flowers

Rama

rangolis

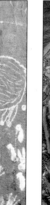

sweets